SCIENCE CORNER

Electricity

Angela Royston

PowerKiDS press™

New York

Published in 2012 by The Rosen Publishing Group Inc.
29 East 21st Street, New York, NY 10010

First Edition

Editor: Katie Powell
Designer: Robert Walster
Picture Researcher: Diana Morris

Library of Congress Cataloging-in-Publication Data

Royston, Angela, 1945-
Electricity / By Angela Royston. — 1st. ed.
    pages cm. — (Science Corner)
Includes index.
ISBN 978-1-4488-5257-4 (library binding)
1. Electricity—Juvenile literature. I. Title.
QC527.2.R685 2012
537—dc22

2010046165

Photographs:
Leslie Garland/Alamy: 13. Wayne Howard/stockphoto: 8.
Brad Killer/istockphoto: 4. Sean Locke/istockphoto: 6. John
Carne Molla/Corbis: 1, 10. Photogenes: 11. Kevin Russ/
istockphoto: 9. Jon Schulte/ istockphoto: 2, 7. Raul
Touzon/National Geographic/Getty Images: front cover.
Tony Tremblay /istockphoto: 5. Voronin76/Shutterstock: 12.
Wayland: 14, 15, 16, 17, 18, 19, 20, 21, 22, 23.

Manufactured in China
CPSIA Compliance Information: Batch #WAS1102PK: For Further Information
contact Rosen Publishing, New York, New York at 1-800-237-9932

Web Sites

Due to the changing nature of Internet
links, PowerKids Press has developed
an online list of Web sites related to
the subject of this book. This site is
updated regularly. Please use this link
to access this list:
http://www.powerkidslinks.com/sc/elec/

Contents

What Is Electricity?

Electricity is used to make things work.
When electricity flows through an electrical
machine, it makes the machine work.

A refrigerator uses electricity to keep food cold.

You cannot see electricity, but you can see what it does. Electricity can be very powerful. It is even strong enough to move trains.

electric lines

Warning! Electricity can be dangerous. An electric shock can kill you.

This train takes electricity from the lines above it.

Using Electricity

People use electricity in their homes. A television set makes sounds and pictures when electricity flows through it.

We use electricity to make light at night. A bulb lights up when electricity flows through it.

Electrical Machines

A kitchen often has several machines that need electricity to work. A microwave oven and a refrigerator both work using electricity.

Can you see which machines in this kitchen need electricity to work?

Electricity can make things hot.
For example, an electric iron
gets very hot.

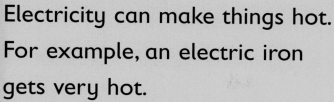

Warning!
An electric iron
stays hot for
a while after
it has been
turned off.

Where Does Electricity Come From?

Electricity is made in power plants. Thick power lines carry electricity away from the power plant. They take it to cities and towns.

As water flows through this dam, it makes electricity.

The power lines are linked to thinner wires. Electricity flows through these wires to different buildings.

power line

In towns and cities, some electric cables and wires are hidden under the ground.

Sockets and Plugs

Wires bring electricity into your home. Electric sockets connect to the wires. When a machine is plugged into a socket, electricity flows through the machine.

Warning!
Do not put anything into an electric socket except a plug that fits it.

Some wires lead to electric lights.
You push the switch to make the
electricity flow. Then the light
comes on!

Batteries

A battery gives a small amount of electricity. Batteries are so small they can fit into objects, such as a toy car or a flashlight. This makes them easy to carry around.

This toy car runs on a battery that fits into the back of the car.

Some batteries are round and some are square. You have to use the battery that fits the toy or machine.

This remote control uses two AA batteries.

A Simple Circuit

A simple circuit uses electricity from a battery. A circuit is a path that allows electricity to flow all the way around it.

As electricity passes through the bulb, the bulb lights up.

wire

wire

bulb

battery case

A simple circuit can have a buzzer
instead of a bulb. As electricity passes
through the buzzer in this circuit,
the buzzer makes a noise.

buzzer

battery case

Making a Circuit

You can make a simple circuit with a battery, a bulb, and two wires. Use the wires to connect the battery to the bulb.

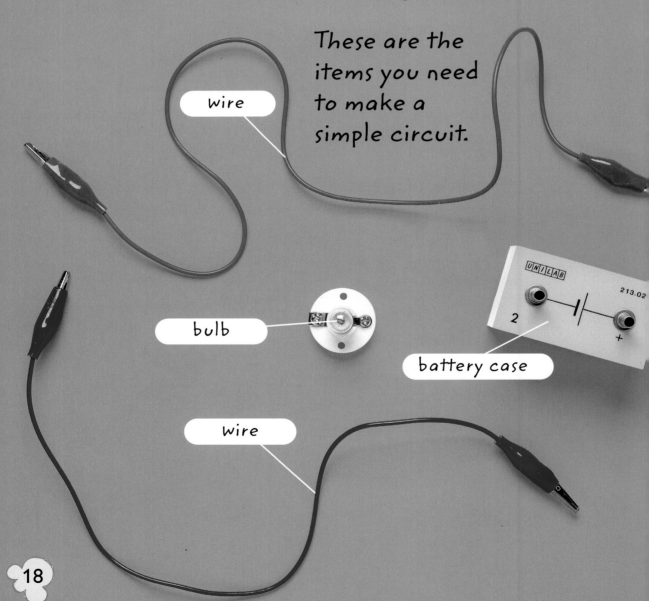

wire

These are the items you need to make a simple circuit.

bulb

battery case

wire

If the circuit is not connected correctly, the electricity will not flow. One of the wires in this circuit is not attached to the bulb, so the bulb will not light up.

Switches

A switch opens and closes a circuit. When the switch is closed, electricity flows around the circuit. The bulb lights up.

Every electrical machine has a switch to turn it on and off.

bulb

switch

battery case

When the switch is open, electricity
cannot flow around the circuit.
The bulb goes off.

Make Your Own Switch

You will need:
- a battery
- a bulb
- two wires
- a paper clip

Follow these simple steps to make a switch.

1. Set up a simple circuit using a battery, a bulb, and two wires.

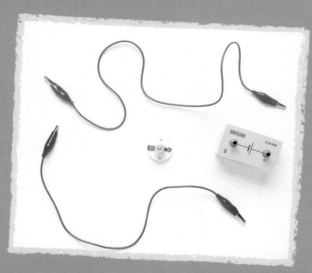

2. Undo one of the wires to the bulb. What happens?

3. Attach the end of the wire to a paper clip.

4. Now touch the screw on the bulb with the paper clip. What happens?

You have a made a switch!

Glossary and Further Information

battery a sealed packet of chemicals that make electricity

cable a thick rope of wires

circuit an unbroken path that electricity can flow around

electricity a form of energy that is used to work electrical machines

power station a building in which electricity is made

socket a set of holes that link a plug to wires carrying electricity

switch a device for turning the flow of electricity on and off

Books

Fun Science Projects: Understanding Electricity
by Gary Gibson
(Stargazer Books, 2009)

Science Alive: Electricty
by Terry Jennings
(Saunders Book Company, 2009)

Science Everywhere: Electricity
by Clint Twist
(Newforest Press, 2010)

Index